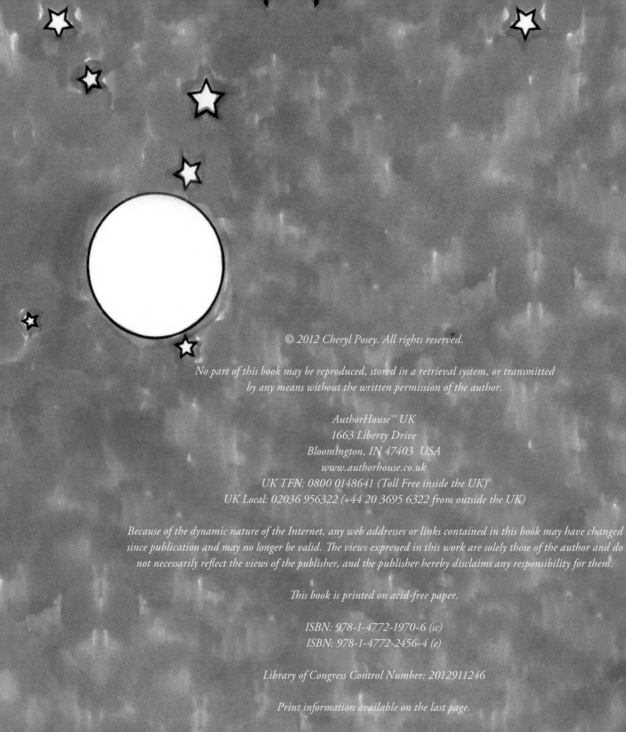

AuthorHouse™ UK
1663 Liberty Drive
Bloomington, IN 47403 USA
www.authorhouse.co.uk
UK TFN: 0800 0148641 (Toll Free inside the UK)
UK Local: 02036 956322 (+44 20 3695 6322 from outside the UK)

Because of the dynamic nature of the Internet, any web addresses or links contained in this book may have changed
since publication and may no longer be valid. The views expressed in this work are solely those of the author and do
not necessarily reflect the views of the publisher, and the publisher hereby disclaims any responsibility for them.

This book is printed on acid-free paper.

ISBN: 978-1-4772-1970-6 (sc)
ISBN: 978-1-4772-2456-4 (e)

Library of Congress Control Number: 2012911246

Print information available on the last page.

Published by AuthorHouse 04/05/2022

authorHOUSE

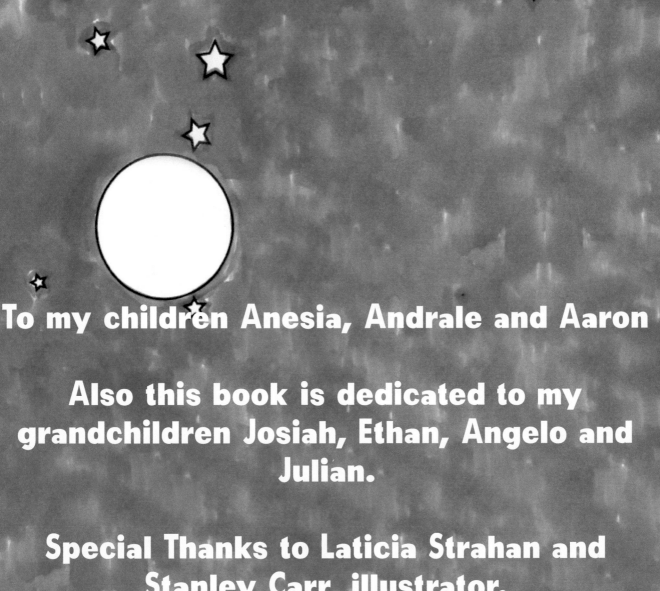

To my children Anesia, Andrale and Aaron

Also this book is dedicated to my grandchildren Josiah, Ethan, Angelo and Julian.

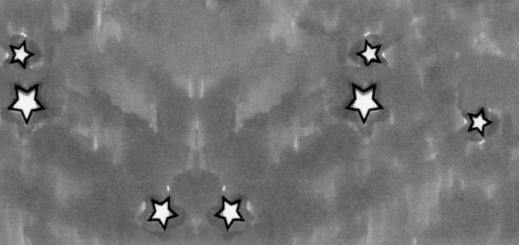

Special Thanks to Laticia Strahan and Stanley Carr, illustrator.

Thank you Lord.

With all of me, I will praise the Lord, You are very great.
You are dressed in the clothes of kings. Psalms 104: 1-3.

The clouds carry You with the wings of the wind, and they bring Your message. Your ministers are like a blazing fire. Psalms 104: 4.

LET THERE BE

GOD'S WORD

Lord, the way You made the earth, it will never be moved. Psalms 104: 5.

Lord, You covered the earth with the high waters.

Psalms 104:6

When You spoke, the water ran quickly down the mountains into the valley, just where You wanted it to go. Psalms 104:7-9

The water that ran into the valley, gives drink to the animals who lives there. Psalms 104:10-11.

The birds also live by the water and they sing their songs.
Psalms 104:12.

The fruit and the vegetables we eat, grow because of the water You have given us. Psalms 104:13-14.

Lord, You gave us all kinds of trees. Psalms 104:15-16.

Trees for food and the birds can live in them too.

Psalms 104:17.

Lord, You made the high hills for the wild goats to live on.

Psalms 104: 18.

You gave us the moon for the four seasons. It tells us when it is winter, spring, summer and fall. The sun knows where to go at all times. Psalms 104:19.

You made the dark night when many of the animals
hunt for food. The Lions roar when they hunt.

Psalms 104:20-21.

Lord, You knew just what to do when You created the earth and everything in it. Psalms 104:24.

The waters so wide and so deep are where the big and small fish live, along with other sea creatures.

Psalms 104:25.

The big ships sail on the sea too. Psalms 104:26.

Lord, You can feed everything You made in the sea. If they are not fed, they cannot live. Psalms 104:27-29.

Lord, You will always be here. You are so very great and the earth knows this about You. Psalms 104: 30-32.

We will sing and talk about You, how good and strong You are. Psalms 104:33-34.

We will praise You and be glad. Psalms 104:35.

Printed in the United States
by Baker & Taylor Publisher Services